# She Saw Me and Said So

## Steve Abhaya Brooks

# Contents

6

**She Saw Me and Said So**

She said, "Hey, Steve, when you begin to write, you become spiritual,"
I'd never thought anything like that before, so I thought about it, I went
back to the moment it began, saw an empty mind, no thought, I looked at
the spirit in the room, I let seeing do the looking, I saw the cars on the
street, I saw the people in the room, "So that's what spiritual feels like,
acceptance, without face or name."

**The Rains Came**

We grew tired from pumping the basement, the rains came
and did not stop, we pumped the flood to the street, the stream
kept coming, cruel Sisiphus, being punished for cruelty, we're
not cruel, the rain kept coming, baling the rain, bucket after bucket,
making the bed each morning, washing my face, brushing my hair,
going outside, greeting the new day, Camus imagined Sisyphus
smiling, I imagine Camus smiling, his rock nearby, pushing the
rock of imagination, it is what we do, we push, we watch the
rock roll back down to the base of the mountain, the rain stops.

## The Crow Caws

In Cocteau's Orphée, the famed poet asks his oldest friend
what to do, "Astonish us," his friend replies, but as an old
poet, nothing astonished him, I'm astonished to be living,
life itself astonishes, what to make of this astonishment, so
commonly borne among us, grass grows, crows fly, the earth
revolves, amazement is cast upon the sea, stupefied, I thunder,
I lightning, I'm shocked with wonder, I cry out, some crows alight
on a narrow branch, one crow caws, life's wonder is a bird song.


## I Stare into the Unknown

I stare into the unknown in the midst of all things known here
on earth, in a cafe on a Monday after registering my new car, used,
small, a hybrid, blue, foreign, I bought the car from my companion,
I sit inside it like I've sat inside so many cars before it, I drive down
the street like so many streets I have driven down before, I drive the
busy streets, I fill an empty chair, I'm crowded with sights, I drive
into the unknown in the midst of all things known, here on earth.

**I Saw a Gun on a Wall**

I saw a gun on a wall, where we all gave blood to save others' lives,
when I thought of owning a gun, I thought I might think to use it,
this was after years in the city, where crime was common and
well-known, "Give us your money, motherfucker," two men said,
they ruined the night, then, "Give us your money, motherfucker...
he's got a gun or a knife," "Get your story straight," I thought,
 "a gun or a knife?" but I said nothing,

I looked at a tree, not far up the street,  "I could just be there,"
I thought, I gave them my last four bucks, they threw my billfold
on the ground, "Fuck this!" the bars were letting out, a lovely night,
the bus driver said, "Get in," there was a serial killer in the city, I was
his target, my house was set on fire, my car was stolen, I never had a
gun, "If I had a gun," I thought, "what would've happened to my
brilliant night?"


**To Be At Ease**

To be at ease in a life of no ease, is to be, one day, at ease,
I take for granted what is, I find 'at ease' to be my barest grant,
I find artificial means for being at ease to be artificial, ease stays
by the heart, by the bone, in the soul, at home, permanently, Keats
called death sweet and easeful, he meant that sense of life we call
death, the endorphin of death is life, buried in plain sight, in the body,
I unearth my finest ease in restfulness, in slow time, the time for peace,
grave concern awakens joy, laughter, the taking of my deepest breath,
to be at ease in a life of no ease, is to be, one day, at ease.

**Not the Enemy**

Not the enemy of the creative, peace is its unmet lover, no one
mocks the blackbird's plumage, the sun never disappoints the beach,
sad eyes, a twinkle in the shadows, set free by the fresh morning light,
I fall into love and discover gravity works in all directions, remembering
old loves, watching old train wrecks, car crashes, airplane dives, to love
so much, I fall in love with love itself, the love of nothing, flowers are
made to seem beautiful by the hand of beauty itself, the leaves on the
trees have found fame, basking in the sun, until the fall, when a tree
is freshly cut down, it exhales the scent of its love.


**Love Came Suddenly**

Love came suddenly upon me when I was outside, cutting the grass,
love lights one candle with another candle, which lights the first candle,
on this dark day in politics, the sun came out, and stayed out, all day,
convinced that love is all, when I go into love, there is nowhere else,
melancholy, fruitful love of sadness, a half-full glass, overflows with
loneliness, the companionship of oneself when love has gone unseen,
indestructible love is the only constancy we leave to live our lives.

## I Fall into Love

I fall into love the way I do, doing corrupts my graceful fall, tears fall from welling eyes to cheeks to the heart from which they're realized, I cannot like what I do not love, I love broadly, I like as much, bare branches crosshatch the sky, etching between here and eternity, a faint heart drifts to the floor, like a body in the ocean of air, I step, as if in a meadow, in a city of missing meadows, walking down the road of my dreams, taking steps inside myself, barefoot, I hesitate to say I love, I stop breathing when I'm outside it, the ground is soaked with rain, birds have gone somewhere dry, the sky is flooded.

## No Words

No words, no words, thought without words, as startling light assumes the air, I found a series of letters that changed my memory from dark to light, I lower my head in a gesture of grief, a kind of forgiveness, I embrace others with inexpressible love, and love speaks for me, I look at others, I can't tell them my love leaps out into them, at the end of the day, my hands rest quietly at the ends of my arms.

## A Happy Lover

I thought I was a happy lover, when all I was, was love itself,
Jesus said, "I am the son of God, now you say it," but no one did,
I've read every poet there is, or a fair approximation, I feel like
a monk sipping tea inside an empty universe, I try to be humble,
but trying always fails and I'm humbled, there is a small bird
like me, on a branch in a tree, about to sing.


## We Are Lovers

"I'm a talker, I'm not a talker," I say to myself, silently, we are lovers,
living somewhat apart, making the distance disappear, we celebrate
the quiet moments of uncelebrated life, our tiny corner of the world
becomes its center, I assume glories that used to thrill me, like blinking
in the sunlight, the steady rain falls on city cement, buildings seem to
sprout up anew, I squelch a yawn in front of a bull, grazing nearby,
no fence between, do not talk me out of my wealth, this vast stillness
in greatest silence.

## Young Outcasts

Young outcasts huddle against the sky, plotting their revenge
with laughter, a holy man puts into practice what others can
barely recall, my head lowers to my chest as the sun sinks
beneath the horizon, spring is on its way, clouds climb into
the lake, huddle under the cover of windy waves, flowers
on the mountains, whiskers on a cat tickle the laughing sky,
Buddha is old Jesus, balder, fatter, grown weary of religion.


## Table in the Light

Table in the light, invitation to write, to chat, to sit at peace,
I imagine my face at peace, it overcomes my eyes, nose and
mouth, I witness the world, angry, spiteful, filled with hate,
spewing bile, I witness my heart filling with these dark motives,
then empty of them, my empty heart, full of itself, joyful cavern
of earthly delight, table in the light, invitation to write, to chat,
to sit at peace.

## Dandelion Teeth

"I'm a solitary," I said to the circle of others, planting their feet
in my heart, "it's not normal for me to be here with you," and
they danced in my limbs, "I choose to be alone, even in public,"
and they swam in my blood, "It's always been like this," I said,
and they breathed the air that fills my lungs, I have no plans for
others, I have no plan for this life that lives me, roses live with
orchids, their common soil, just as fertile, feeds them both.

## Very Little is Spoken

Very little is spoken of joy, or its remainder, happiness,
joy is buried in the moment like gold, to be discovered,
unearthed, the moment flows by like a stream, a river,
a current, a trickle, a trickle of sun, a trickle of ocean,
a trickle of mountains, very little spoken of joy, so
ordinary, so commonplace, very little said of happiness,
joy's ongoing revolution, I find hidden joy in words,
I speak them aloud and they become me.

**Thinking of Death**

Once I began thinking of death, I continued to live, life goes on,
I saw my grandpa in his casket, pappy in tears, I thought of death,
mother's mother died, she was here, then gone, it was her dying
prayer, I cried at my father's funeral, my mother told me to speak up,
"I'm good at this," I said, emotions come, I love the rush of feeling,
the love of others brings out the tears, death deftly prompts the love
that's here, death is a recognition, in ourselves, of another's life in
ours, my death is like another life in mine, one I love and cry for,
I celebrate one I barely know, he touches me deep as any other.


**My Friend Fell from His Roof**

He lay on the ground, his phone in the house, no one might have
heard him yell, lying in pain, he called out, a woman with her dog
called 911, he can't recall the siren, going to the hospital, or much
else, at a ripe age, he became a dancer, there was dried blood on his
lips, "It hurts when I laugh," he said, laughing, two nurses, a doctor
knew him, if they patch him up, he might limp, I suggested a story,
a neighbor's child is about to be attacked by a vicious dog, he leaps
off the roof, breaks his hip, saves the child, all in a day's work, I'd just
read a story of Napoleon's invented heroics, "Isn't this life interesting,"
he said and laughed, "it hurts when I laugh," I kissed his forehead
and said, "It's good to love a friend, after a fall."

## I Face the Poet

I face the poet, her voice containing volumes of matchless beauty,
there are those among us with joy made eminently translatable,
you see them walking, with smiles, with twinkling eyes, shaded
by the weather, such a simple solution to the world's woes,
children know it well, her words were a kind of listening,
spoken with eyes wide open.


## There Was a Time

There was a time when I did not fit in myself, I could not
be folded, too much muscle, weight, thickness, too big a body,
too many visions, now I can wrap myself in myself like an egg,
like an absent thought, I have become smaller and bigger in the go,
made in the unmaking, nothing in me seeks to fill out the world,
to make it my body's whorl, unpacked, unfurled, the packing
in the box is gone, the box is missing.

## I Linger in the Shower

I linger in the shower when I habitually hurry through, hotter-
than-usual water makes my eyes rise to the horizon, I look beyond
the curtain to a peacefulness I feel in my ease, my spine is caressed
by torrents of waterfall, liquid sunfire, else, I think of trivial matters,
like cleansing my body with soap, my body is cleansed, regardless,
I am uplifted in the bargain, I look up, look down, look all around,
the water can't tell the difference.


## In Memory

In memory, I search the past to teach the moment I'm living now,
to find some time that reminds me how I might expect to feel, then
do, to retrieve the present from the storehouse of the past, I call it up,
I glean the past and future to feed the present time, we suckle life.

## After Death

After death, I will lose the habit of thought, yet live on,
free of mind, it is a challenge to contemplate the absence
of contemplation, tossing babies out with the water, knowing
they have come from the same source, I enter the absence
of contemplation, then return to it.

## Cats Dance

I don't have to write a poem, there's no law, I don't have to
feel good, I can wallow in despair, if that's my desire, even if
there is no desire, the sun is shining, it's a lovely day, people
are smiling, cats dance, I've never seen a cat dance, but I can
say I have, I am human, I'm stuck in my head, making up
stories, all there is available, or so I think, thinking thinks
like that, I begin to breathe, in and out, in and out, fresh air
kills old thinking, I breathe in and out, I act as if I am life
itself, I begin to live again, it's a lovely day, people are
smiling, the sun is shining, cats dance.

## The Age of Appearance

Cutting the grass while it's still wet, it clings to rubber wheels,
to my shoes, I stop short, the front yard is good enough for visitors
who are due, I find a use for an old towel, wiping the grass from
my wet shoes, keeping up appearance is no small task in this age
of appearance, everyone is beautiful, or at least, well-attended-to,
we are all on stage, these days, we make movies of ourselves, life
has become a selfie, we're on film, appearance is the film of reality,
wet grass clings to my shoes, our worst criminals are coiffed, dressed
to the nines, their teeth are capped and white, refugees wear shirts
from fashion lines,they have cell phones, starving children die.

## At the Ballet

At the ballet, the first dancer is great, the second even greater,
the first dancer is technically superb, the second seems magical,
she seems not to dance but to appear in one place after another,
she's fluid light, a body without a body, like thought without
thought, then she is absorbed by the company, I recall another
time, I went to see my good friend's lover dance in a famous
company, all the dancers were excellent, I was impressed, then
she came on stage, I took a deep breath, there was a dramatic
change in the atmosphere, who can say what the difference is
between doing something well and art, birds fly, eagles soar,
we are lifted above the ground, we join the sky.

## At 17, Late at Night, in Bed

At 17, late at night, in bed, I looked at the space between thoughts,
there was nothing there, not the nothing of something missing but
the nothing of everything present, I was God, but there was no
God, I blasphemed my emptiness, no one talked of such things,
I forgot about it, but it never left, the emptiness of the mind,
between all thoughts, became my legacy.


## Kabir Says

Kabir says, "Lift the veil that obscures the heart," and I hear
my heart sing, the exuberance of the spirit, rhyme that, verse that,
scan that, poet, beyond the glass, trees seem to be chattering madly
to each other, I look down, I see I am a boat, I look and all I see is
sea, I fall in love with my self when I see there is no one on board.

## I Gaze Down at the Palms of My Hands

I gaze down at the palms of my hands and I see what sets
my heart free, energy is a dull word for dynamic eternity
that opens my heart to yours, if I defend myself with pride
and invective, I know the culprit, call this villain ego,
he disappears as soon as I call him out, behind his
machinations, a squirrel in a cage runs inside circles,
clouds of dust, a squealing voice, nowhere to go,
around and around, I gaze down at the palms
of my hands, I gaze at the life of my hands.


## My Spine Cracks

My spine cracks on the back of the chair, a tree's limbs twist,
seeking the sun, old man sways as he walks, moving each leg
gingerly, learning new ways, great soul in small bodies, our
bodies at sea in a solar system, the ball skims the field, foot
to foot to foot to goal, free hands applaud, between poems,
a gulf, as great as the Grand Canyon, that majestic divide.

## All at Once in Moving

I make my way to peaceful places in the midst of turmoil and grief,
my secret, I am human, living in a body, on earth, in time, all the trees
turn green again, as if they stopped waiting for some command, a tiger
comes near, the river speaks uncertain babble in my ear, all at once,
in moving, I am still, all at once, in stillness, I move.


## The Rain Falls

The rain falls, in torrents, sheets, drops, a congregation,
a flock, the rain floods, turns the lawn to a pond, the yard
to a lake, cheers to fears, the rain, like the reign of a king,
overrules the people with dictates, a sprinkle becomes a
deluge, what's needed becomes unwanted fate, indoors,
by the fire, we count the days since we last saw warming
sun, the rain stops, on its own, as if it had a heart, as if
the light does, we give heart to what beats down on us,
blaze or blight, we express the heart.

## In the House on Molimo Street

In the house on Molimo Street, I woke with a twinkle
in my eye, my life at the time was a misery, it was dark,
or so I thought, when I saw the twinkle, I knew misery
was merely passing through, I saw a flicker of brilliance,
and I knew I was still in the heart of delight.


## I Sat Beside a Lake

When I was four, I sat beside a lake with my mother, I was grim,
there was room for me to be grim in my young life, room to feel
sad, I was laughed at, I was guided into laughter, I was taught to
laugh, this is a grim, sad world, guided into laughter, guided into
war, I'm free to laugh, free to laugh at myself, free to laugh at war,
I've lived long enough to see the fields come back to life, green
again.

**Breath Stops Awhile**

Breath stops awhile in my chest before taking it over in full,
there is a brief physical moment to the moment of life itself,
a gasp in the grasp of joyfulness that, prideless, speaks a
moment of pride, these are words I give to what overcomes me, on a warm Tuesday night.

**In This World of Turmoil**

In this world of turmoil, in the path of a raging tornado, take shelter,
ignore its destruction, hide in plain sight, live without fear, a squirrel
crosses the road, on its way somewhere, its chances the same, it cannot
direct the traffic, cannot stay at home, cannot let fear rule, my lovers red,
red lips, the same as a tiger's blood, the same as mine, as Jack Spicer
warned the poets, "Whatever you say, you must say what comes next."
I say the sun is out, the rain has gone, the trees are thick with leaves.

**I Write a Poem**

I write a poem, get ready for yoga, get ready for life, ready or not,
readiness exists, what begins begins, ready or not, my routine is a
blank slate, an open door, an empty mind, begin, as the clock ticks,
time is silent, creeping on cat feet, ready to leap, my father taught
me to love a great shower with a strong, steady stream, I found
one, in a shaded glen near my hut at the YMCA.


**I Remember Yesterday's Joy**

I remember yesterday's joy, in the same chair, by the same window,
in imitation, I try to experience the same sense of joy, and that fails,
so I seek to follow the way joy seemed to have occurred, failing that
path, I surrender my actions, I let "no one" be, and "no one" takes my
place, "no one" feels my joy, "no one" succeeds at my job, joy occurs
in itself, anf then it occurs in its recognition, a fire truck wails out
its sweet song, like a loon, crossing the lake.

## I'm Attracted to the Crazies

I'm attracted to the crazies with stringy hair, talking to no one,
those uninterested in acceptance, wandering the streets like gardens,
sanctioned by our desire to be free, condemned by our imprisonment,
the crow, the crab, the dog, the tiger in the jungle, looking for food,
I look in their faces for wisdom, but none comes, they are a facade,
there is a meadow called spirit that is free for the free to wander.


## Thatched Roof

The first thatched roof that I ever lived under was this sad, battered
head, I stayed for a time in a palapa on Holbox, Quintana Roo, it was
an island like this head, on a neck from the mainland's body, a peaceful
place, surrounded by peaceful waters, except during storms, I was there
with a woman, my companion for a while, no longer, a sandy isle, with
a quiet population, until TV came, soap operas took over the island, we
traveled to India, where without media, I emptied my head of theatrics,
thoughts were clear, people everywhere, my palapa remains crowded
with footsteps, I rest on sand by the sea in the Holbox of my India.

## Matisse at a Sidewalk Table

Matisse sits at a sidewalk table wearing ear buds, reading tech
books, he looks up the street and grins, giggles at his iphone, rocks
back and forth, I stopped painting before I moved here, my lover is a
painter, I encourage her, she attends modeling sessions, I like what she
does, as if she is doing the painting for us, I share it with her, much of
the world does what I love doing, I encourage their joy, others' love of
what I love rains love in my heart when my heart is open, a torrential
downpour floods the dry riverbed, causing it to flow, if Matisse stops
painting, but his heart is full, is he not still Matisse?


## 222 is My Lucky Number

222 is my lucky number, I used to live at that address, many unfortunate
things occurred at that time, little did I care, I cared deeply, and still do,
but little did I care, it was a time, in my attempt to be carefree, I became
careless and uncaring, I buried care in those days, it unearthed itself,
came back to life, my room was a dark crypt for caring kept in a light
sarcophagus, perhaps that remembered number held caring safe for
another life, I left my bed to risk my well-being, returned, sometimes
unwell, what is well when wellness remains at the core, in its secret
haven, wellness returns to the unwell when caring is given back its life.

## Great Truths are Buried

Great truths are buried in simple truth, we love greater than
what we love, knife, fork, spoon stand for various parts of our
lives, along with the plate, Emily Dickinson said of the truth,
"Tell it slant," Catch 22, a friend said, "You start one direction,
then reverse yourself," with no plan, there can be no reverse,
no direction, no way to go, everything gets from here to here,
from dinner plate to exhilarate, happiness is revolutionary, I love,
even like, myself, to like oneself is to admit one is like oneself,
in every way, I am like myself in every way, with no difference
between us, I am neither superior nor inferior to who I am,
we're the same, happiness is inherent, open to the apparent.


## Killing Time

I wander through the house, looking for nothing, wasting time,
killing time, these expressions are wrong, disengagement from
purpose frees wonder, the first poem I ever had published was
called, "I Love to Wander," I was in 7th Grade in my new school,
a photograph was taken, I was given to wandering, I was given
to wonder, wonder is freed by wandering, my young mind would
wander free to be, deep in wonder, at the dinner table, mother
would call me, "Stephen," then my brothers, then my father,
"Hey, where were you?" I was wandering in nowhere,
wandering in wonder, nourishing time.

## We Light Candles

We light candles in the daytime, we turn out the lights at night, we
sleep, what interests me are those who dwell alone, content to shine,
unheralded, a thousand saints go unnoticed in the world, unnamed by
their acclaim, a million songs are sung softly to no one's ear, they drift
in the air, love wanders silent from heart to heart or else remains behind
closed doors, I stop before the verse is done, to see its source in stillness,
thriving, sunlight settles on a leaf that spreads itself wide in the light.


## Profound Instincts

I don't usually wear this shirt, it seems too nice for daily display,
I polish my shoes, my feet feel better, cause and effect unclear,
cold skin, I wear half-gloves, doctor says I have veins missing in
my hands, I hear the Mississippi River may reach an all-time crest
this week, in the cafe, one man shaved his beard, another has grown
his out full, the weather's turned hot, that's really all you need to hear,
more and this might seem profound, thanks to your profound instincts.

## I Applied to My Life

"Why don't you apply in poetry, you're writing poems all the time,"
she said so, because she had seen me doing what I had been doing,
I kissed her and hugged her and applied to my life, I went on in its
direction, I awakened to my awakening, I followed my following,
the grasses of the prairie lean in the direction of sun and wind.


## If the Moon Had Eyes

If the moon had eyes, it would see the earth in a woeful compromise,
if the moon had eyes, it would see the demise of the earth's condition,
if the moon had eyes, it would close its eyes and blink at the blighted
sight, if the moon had eyes, it would see the sun's heat turn oven on
earth, if the moon had eyes, it would weep but not for the earth's
eternity, the moon has nothing to lose, the sun is safe, it's our life
that's in decline, the children of those who walked on the moon
may suffer their time on earth, "save yourselves, no one else will,"
the moon would say, if it had lips to speak.

## Weeping in the Heart

Weeping has come up in my heart, where it thrives in
the joy of bereavement, saying something is not the same
as doing, but the doing of saying is, some brittle thought,
held in the mouth, softens into a kind of morsel, finding
food in the heart where it's always been, a cache of caring.

## In Praise of Age

In the full flower of my youth, I did not care to listen to age,
at sixty, I rode past the factory where I worked as a young man,
I could see myself standing at a table of steel teeth, stacking them,
from there I saw myself ride a bicycle along the river road, my
glimpse from then to then and back again was brief and briefly
knowing, history seemed dense, at the time, time has thinned out
its memory, what I could not see then, I see now, clearly, sadly,
with sweet concern, I forgive my youth for its thick, clouded
inexperience, I leaped from caged youth to riding my bike
in the sun beside the wide Mississippi.

## The Wall

I come to stare at the wall, to see what I don't see, the wall's gift,
to think of nothing is to think of nothing else, to let thought go free,
this is my place of caring in the midst of a vast uncaring world, when
caring is untethered from cares, it returns to the source it bears, I stare
at the empty wall of space in a public place, and I'm free to see the pain
and joy in the faces that pass the wall, the old man with baggy pants,
old bones, like mine, he sits carefully down, he drinks his tea and thinks
of eternity with a smile, soft hat on his head, shoes big for his feet, he
talks to the universe, never leaves his body, he remains at peace in his
fleshy shell.

## Food For All

A guardian of life's effect, ego gets me less present in life, I look
at the sky to see if my eyes are clear, at the ground to see the ground,
I listen to Bob Dylan to orient myself in time and place, I attend a poetry
reading given by young women, I hear a true language, different from
my own, yet we are all poets, I remember being as bold, as afraid,
among my once-young peers, ego finds a place or ignores its place,
the sky finds itself grounded, Dylan sings, "Gotta serve somebody,"
he serves himself, he serves everyone, earth appropriates the sky,
drinks it dry, then serves up food for all.

## I am Taciturn

Taciturn, I seldom smile, when laughter was my way before this time,
several women taught me to speak, many men showed me how to talk,
a guru asked me, "What is the secret," I said, "There is no secret,"
there is only secrecy, we withhold wisdom from each other, we lie,
with no secrets, why speak, except to end secrecy or help it thrive,
I returned what I learned, until I learned to be still, silent, at peace,
however, the noisy thoughts in my mind continue to raise their
voices, to curtail the blather of my mind I ignore its insistence, so
be still, busy world, and see yourself at peace, that is the secret.

## Peace is Vagrant

Peace is vagrant in my body, I am vagrant in the same body,
and when I breathe deep, I gather myself, I give myself a safe
home, I read the language of others, their violent, vagrant images,
a small boy does windmills in his mother's face, he grins and jumps
about, a dog trainer touches the neck of a volatile dog, the dog stops,
the man is called wise by the unpeaceful owner of the unpeaceful dog,
wisdom is a touch, a choice of words, a deep breath, a way of being,
breathe, breathe, I tell myself, tame the vagrant beast, breathe in
the wind.

## The Heart of the Rose

I wonder when it started, this trait of stopping to be the roses,
I wrote an autobiography of the rose that senses itself, to look
around with brightly-colored eyes, to see, with thorns in my side,
I was a sensitive boy, no different than being a human child, one
day I fell in roses, and scratched, I met the love of beauty and pain,
the next day I saw my family as roses and my place among them, I
saw roses throughout, still wary of thorns, I saw beauty and pain,
I am beauty and pain, blood red and sharp, a bouquet of spectacle,
I fell among roses and became one of them in their beauty and pain.


## Love Walks Onto the Battlefield

Love walks onto the battlefield untouched by men, unseen as love,
I look for love in daily life, listen for its nearly silent voice, what
sound do I make in my politics, my poetical musings, I put my heart
into its remembered place of love, something occurs on this battlefield
of thoughts, can I hear love's footsteps, can I be love, when the things
that I love define love, is love complicit with itself, are there signs
of love in war, before, during, after, I think I see it there.

**The Sparrow**

I have regained some of the magic of my life from its youthful
spree, blind optimism in my youth, neither blind nor optimistic now,
I've slowed down enough to achieve the speed of my heart, the goal
of time, what I approximated when young, came true in natural being,
I like who I am, in being what I am, in what I am being, this is not
the result of aging, but aging has revealed it so, once the magic
of the real, I'm now the real of the magic, a common sparrow
on a common branch, being a sparrow on a branch, flies.


**Heartbreaking Love**

Many times I have been in heartbreaking love with many a presence,
the presence I called loving has faded but not its reality, the older I get,
the sharper the pangs of physical love appear, a feeling of gratitude
soothes the sweet pain of remembered pleasure, it's said that memory
prepares us for the present, collapsing time, what once was, is here now,
to show here and now what continues to be, the past is gone, gone, and
gone again, leaving timelessness free to breathe on its own.

**The Key**

I have found the key to folly and cruelty, but it solves nothing,
solution is found in the opposites of folly and cruelty, some care
to institute their solution, and left on their own, they flourish,
death is a solution, but what is death, a surrender without care,
here, in living life before death, the key to surrender is wonder,
in the face of folly and cruelty, wonder is acceptance, surrender
and acceptance are different from capitulation, true wonder does
not miss reality, no dream, it flies to essence, wonder flies to
the essence of my heart, very like a bird flies home.


**Seeing My Brother Again**

I'm looking at my dead brother, not him, of course, a similar man,
same build, hair, eyes, wrinkles, mouth, hands, nose, style of clothing,
same demeanor, this man is younger, fitter, cleaner, with shorter hair,
he seems saner, his expressions the same, the same face and skin,
a ringer, his gentle smile touches my heart, I see my brother, happy,
alive, this man turns his back, I can't see his face, the same as my
brother did, my brother killed himself, estranged from those who
knew him before, this man leaves the cafe, metaphor for an abrupt
departure, it was good to see my brother again, after these last painful
years, to see the good in a man who found his way in music and death.

**I Love the Life of My Hands**

I love the life of my hands, my emissaries in the world, they do
the work required, sometimes they defy that work on their own,
in the field, hands know better than the mind, they intuit its thought,
hands are facts, mind imaginary, the heart a go-between, my heart
runs to my hands, my hands run to my heart, my mind spins in place,
the actions of my hands have little to do with their explanation, explain
yourself, I say, and my hands rise in the gesture of a shrug, my hands
do the bidding of my tongue, my heart, my mind, reluctantly, I love
my hands, they seem to have a life of their own, they play at work.


**To My Friend Who Has Died**

At our reunion he demanded I never change and I agreed, what will
never change is our startled friendship, I long respected him, in school,
I took him as one of the toughs who lived down by the river, he admired
me, I admired him, it was a natural bond, we disagreed about politics,
yet we never sparred in anger, the false distance between us, never
there, has finally disappeared.

## I'm Fearful for a Woman

I'm fearful for the woman who talks to herself, she does it outloud,
we all talk to ourselves, I talk to myself, I do it in silence, this one
blows the game open, she talks to others no longer present, she
catches herself and bites her tongue, other times, she barrels ahead,
when I first saw her, years ago, I thought she might be a poet, she
seemed to have filled a paper napkin with cryptic notes in longhand,
I've spoken a few words to her, over the years, I speak to others,
I speak silent words of stillness to an unseen public, in private.


## The Spirit in the Room

The spirit in the room, across which bodies move, among which
some love, silent and invisible to most, that spirit appears to a few,
some may call it God, it is what's often called God, but God it is not,
else the air is God, feeling, seeing is God, space is God, time is God,
everything God, through which everything passes, itself among itself,
so be it, but I cannot then call it by a name, or else I make it small.

## The Faces in the Cafe

The faces of men and of women grace this place of common
commerce, every face is its own, grown distinct by life's sculpting
hand, soft and hard, some light shines within, less or more divine
or profane, who can say which, a mask of ornamental looks
redefines the light one seems to be, a seer may catch sight of
that which cannot bide its inside on the outside seen, we know
that light is light, regardless of the brilliance or the lack of it,
every face has its light, variations glow from faint to great, they
fit, one need not look for light in others, it will make itself known,
a firefly, a flicker of a flame in the dungeon of the night, you are
a conflagration embanked by lidded eyes, half-closed, unhid.


## I Greeted a Friend

I greeted a friend on her way, her husband dying, any day now,
she was in town to make music, a rehearsal for a performance,
he has been rehearsing his passing for five or six years now,
too soon, a victim of Agent Orange in his youth, soldiering
for America, his courage has been evident throughout his
life and remains today, his body eaten alive from the inside,
no bullets did the damage, he survived war, came home to a
gradual damage, it took years to appear, she and I exchanged
pleasantries, no use decrying the unspoken, he became a maker
of ovens, bread, and children, thriving in love, his wife makes
music during the upending war of imminent death, her wide
smile opens with light the darkness that often goes unlit.

## In the Mission District, San Francisco

I stood on the corner in the Mission where I had been
the day before, I looked at the same world, similar people,
it had changed, I changed it, one day, I saw through misery's
eyes, the next, it seemed a joyful place, the world had changed
in twenty-four hours, the same sun shone brightly down, some
tragedy had been erased in time, or some fortune had been found,
nothing I remembered comprised the difference, one day to the other,
I accept the light and the shade, happy or sad, it was the same street.


## Flying from Hong Kong

Flying from Hong Kong, half-asleep, I thought, fear is not real,
love is real, I am called Fearless, yet I'm afraid, I'm fearless, born
and bred in fear, fear is the tenor of the times, I am timeless, I've
lived in times of love, I've lived in fear, fear comes up in me like
weather, I am climate, I came to this outside table to escape a
loud voice that followed, I can get used to anything but fear,
love alters fear's presence, I love this fearful world, fear forgets
love, love forgets nothing, I love, love inside fear grows small,
fear inside love turns to something gently seen, I'm a serious man,
love takes off my glasses, my eyes soften, passing cars become a low
rumble, cubes of color, a way to get somewhere, small rooms to die in.

## My Dead Father

My dead father used to appear in my dreams in various despair,
almost comical, but now I might expect something more revealing,
something far reaching, but my dreams have only my memories to
rely on, he, in whom I invested so much, said little I could feel or use,
he was busy seeming a life, not much living it, like absent poetry, how
much he was present in my life is how much I was present in his, I put
my life in him and got myself back, unaffected, the same, yet I love
him, a spark of light will suffice in a vagrant verse.

## Buried in History

Lie buried in history, poet, lay down among the bubbling graves,
if no one heeds your verse, be sleek in your faded remembrance,
go the way of seeds, poke about in the dirt, plant the future trees.

I went to a memorial for a forgotten poet no one there remembered,
I looked around the room, the same was true of the gathered poets'
work, there are a thousand unknown saints for each one known.

**The Wise Crow Sings**

A wise crow among the crows, he learns to be common
because it's true, laying aside his perceptive inclinations,
he clings to the wire, one among many, he marvels at the
common tune, the common tone, he does not claim to be
wise, it goes unrecognized, he is common, after all.

Wisdom is common as well, the undeclared truth fits
the common crow, the wise crow keeps his own counsel,
he keeps the common secret secret, the wise crow sings a
common saw,  sings the truth in every caw, he does not
forget what he does not say, but sings it in a softer lay.


**I Erase My Poems**

I erase my poems as easily as I'll be erased by time, gone
but not forgotten by the blank and empty heart of forever,
what once was, still is, as surely as always lasts an eternity,
these words cannot define the real, any more than time can
be seen, unseen, unbeen to be, there's nothing to fear of fear
in this love unconfined.

## These Words From Nowhere

These words that come from nowhere to here appear,
delight me like the sun that illuminates the leaves on the
trees of spring from which they grow green, these sentences
seek sun, illuminated branches, the unseen seen, the world is
absurd, it has no reason to be, and yet it exists, a tiny sparrow
hops across the grass, ready to fly if need be, other birds walk,
some birds run, the sparrow hops across the green grass lawn.


## The Poetry Mines

I make my way down into the poetry mines, prospecting for gold,
prepared to dig into the ordinary depths of everyday ore, I forget my
aches and pains, I dig with a golden shovel, I'm a golden yellow canary,
I fly below ground, my death is the hero of my worth, I was born to die,
poetry's gold is its fatal gas, it kills those who find its deep vein, this
is the mortal warning, the search for gold that glitters, open this vein
at your risk, it will end your life as you know it.

## Piling On

Piling on, thoughts keep coming, branches burdened
with leaves reach to the sky, beyond life's death, I imagine
a life with purpose that death enshrines, yet I seek only
to secure my amateur standing as life itself.

## One Drink

"One drink won't kill you," and one poisonous thought won't
turn me evil, stealing a towel won't make me a thief, it merely
begins the practice, picking up a thought inclines me to hold it,
holding a thought, it stays, this mind is trainable, teachable, eager
to take up its habits, a dog, left on its own, will shit on the carpet
and chew up the furniture, it wants to be told what to do, sit, stay,
good boy, it will wag its tail.

**Independence Day**

Half past the hour, way past yesterday, can I get past the past,
walking down the street, soaking up the scenery, the earth underfoot,
paradise a long way off, unless you are standing inside it, consecutive
thoughts, non-consecutive reality, sun on cars, I grew up too soon, then
not soon enough, I arrange myself alphabetically, starting with zephyr,
zebra, a row of birds on a branch, everyone has a life they carry around
with them, mostly inside, I am the master of my fate, fate is my master,
I have no master, police have cordoned off this neighborhood of the
celestial stars, a cigarette hits the pavement, the famous death of a firefly.

**Raindrops Ride the Gravity Slide**

Raindrops ride the gravity slide, stopping beside each
other on earth, I see the same building behind the same
trees, the same sky above them, wonder does not escape
my grasp, it decides, it reinvents my eyes.

## Vocabulary

I made up vocabulary to match the one available, I wanted
to learn all the words I heard, as if it was mine to do, then I
thought about usage, which words were popular, to learn them too,
which should I use, the most and best, or the other, the best-liked,
it's my choice, unrestrained, I invite words to appear at the will
of the page, the democracy of merit and glory, on a blind date,
but neither takes me home, my mind would map the way, but
my heart is the beacon of arrival, my heart tramps the path,
headed for the wilderness, the forest, the jungle.


## When No Poem Comes

When no poem comes, poetry consumes the room, like an absent
love, she, always a she, has just closed the door, leaving her presence
behind, I'd rather be with her, but in her absence, I am still with her,
I become the muse of my muse, calling myself to task, back to life,
back to love, when love has fled, absence can only recall the form,
I imitate love of the poem, but it's only absent love I see, love is
born in love, not in its object, a poem born in love is love, I am
love itself, I was born as a poem, I was born to be.

## My Friend Writes Long Poems

My friend writes long poems, his words roiling, I used to think
that way, silence is filled to the point where silence bursts through
the air's barriers, words are air-painted to look like tsunami walls,
air then seems airless, my friend floods the page with words of air
until silence stands out loudest, silence, the holding pattern of light,
the hands of a mime, a wall, stillness, in the midst of the storm,
peace, in place of the ongoing war.


## I Book a Flight

I book a flight to Seattle to see my children, both adults, times
have changed, they have changed, I have changed, we have
changed, now is a place of change, even though now is
always the same, never changing.

When they were children, we seemed more the same, but change
has changed us, some is good, my son says family is only people
you know all your life, my daughter says she's not so sure about
that, I talk of blood, a kind of physical now, it stays the same,
 it keeps us alike.

Bound by blood, we wander far afield, over time, over the miles,
unconditional love lives in the now, ignoring the differences, love
lives now, despite the changes, across time and miles and inches.

**My Words Sift My Bones**

My heart aches, I sit down to write, knowing this ache is
my guide, if I let it, knowing this aching is fodder for much else,
poetry feed on the aching heart for its appeal, language loves the
company of misery, holding it in esteem, I hold my heart in my
hands, to fist it tight or soothe away its ache, my words open my
fists, they advise a caress, my words sift my bones, this ache is
my guide, heart is its path, I go on without a guide, heartache,
no longer my guide, is left to be loved to its forgiveness.


**Coming Up With A Name**

Hot, painting a house, high above El Cerito, late on a Friday,
Peter and I tried to conjure up a new name for our enterprise,
the one we'd been using, it turned out, had been taken by
someone else, it was hot, it was Friday, someone finally
said, "Paint Your Chicken." That was it, we were done,
time to pack up and go home, **Paint Your Chicken**.

**Carry a Whisper**

Cyclist on the sidewalk in a city where the streets
are dangerous, soft-spoken, caring, in a world where
shouting is common discourse, I carry a whisper into
the cacophony, I practice truth at heart, I make my way
along the crowded thoroughfare, home at the end of day.


**Holding the Hand of the Future**

A child's hand in a mother's hand, holding the hand of the
future, carrying it forward, perhaps no different than what came
before, the possibility of the future touches the skin of the young,
spoken for or against, life lives on, in the flesh of a child, small
hearts grow larger, beat larger, beat in their own way, on their
own path, my mother had dreams for me, meant to be the
fulfillment of her best life, dreams come true as reality, my
life has fulfilled an absence of dreaming, here on the farther
shore, I give thanks for the strong, soft hand that held mine.

**An Alpha Bulldog**

Using its paw, a bulldog tries to dominate the hand that
pets it, it begins to turn the tables, to right the alpha/beta
balance, accepting the attention of betas, alpha dog appears
docile, centuries have selected its sad eyes to win over hearts
and minds, the glum bulldog looks to find a bulldog world
and sees only people, and who pets the human owners
with grins and kind words, asking for their names?


**The Spirit in the Room**

When I say that I look at the spirit in the room, what do I mean,
what does it mean 'to look at', how can I see what is not visible,
to look is to focus, to recognize, to show insight, to look at the
spirit in the room is to first think of nothing else, God is a focal
point in eternity, I set sight on distance, look here, look there,
look nowhere in particular, don't think of a cow, or a crow,
misdirection is another direction, look out for spirit.

## The Sight of Trees

The sight of trees gives me peace, these beasts of the earth,
at peace with the sky, peace has been robbed of its vigorous
place at the center of our lives, the Sequoias, the pines, the
cedar, elm, oak, and their fruited cousins, Buddha sat under
a tree, something happened and nobody knows what, Jesus
was hung on a symbolic tree, lynchings cursed innocent trees,
peace is cursed by the violent, but peace outlasts every storm,
the sight of trees gives me peace, these beasts of the earth,
at peace with the sky.


## I Laze About

Lazy, I laze about in my getting from here to there, I laze about
in my driven nature, something must be the driver, I laze about
in this poem, falling awake on the woodsy words, lazing about
conjures amazement for everything before me, I'm lazy, I laze
about, grazing sheep fatten themselves for slaughter, I'm lazy
in dying, as well, in no hurry, I laze about death, my lazy song
drifts on air, until it fades into the atmosphere.

**Dear Reader**

Cars go fast, faster, bugs hit the screen door, precedent is set, speed
kills, I ride my bike to the soccer game, much slower than years ago,
do you play soccer, do you ride a bike, are you looking over my shoulder,
we're in this together, everything I say, I say to you, dear reader, you are
who I think you are, whoever I think you are, in being who you are.


**I Speak the Earth**

Every day passing is my last day on earth, every day is my first,
this same old earth, I stand on its toes, its limbs, its backside, its
forehead, I look down its nose at its chest, heaving, inhaling, tasting
the wind, in my rumbling, the earth rumbles, in my growth, the earth
changes itself, the earth changes into itself, pulsing, rising, sinking,
spinning, I come from the earth, I return to the earth, in between I
dream big, elements of the earth speak the earth, I speak the earth,
instead of time.

## I Work Out the Details

I work out the details, making a life of the life I've been given,
sometimes I'd rather not, what has been given seems enough,
it's a given, the devil's in the details, so are the angels, tangled
in wire, the wire is why are we here, why am I here, a given,
taking, I take what has been given, as if to make something
more of it, the less I take, the more I recognize the given, the
less I am, the more I am, wires fade, when working these
details is the freeing of the angels.


## A Dear Friend Has Died

A dear friend has died, today, I'm reminded of my father's dying,
my son said of his beloved granddad, it's easier to love him now,
how can someone who was loved in life be more loved in death,
it sounds harsh, but now, nothing stands in the way, now, nothing
clouds the clarity of our loving, clarity was always there, clouded
by uncertainty, uncertain love is our inheritance, death is certain,
love is freed, and of my friend, I say I loved you, then and now,
perhaps more then, but now it becomes more clear.

## One Person's View

Poetry, one person's view of himself through the eyes
of the world, there is the world of others, there is the world
itself, which do I speak? I see the world of others in myself,
I see the world in myself, I see the world of others, confounding,
illuminating, I see the world itself, providential, cruel, a comfort,
a release, the world is my illumination, I am its illuminator, a green
grasshopper becomes my speaking voice, consumed by a bluebird.


## A Store for Sheets

Feeling miserable, I say, "ego," and my misery goes away,
ego proposes thought in mind, but when exposed, it evaporates,
worried, strangled by some problem, I don't solve it, I call it out,
solutions appear in the clear light of absent ego, the mind works,
this is no philosophy, like taking a fast-acting aspirin, better, this
is saying the word, boo, to a ghost in a sheet, a ghost appears,
I say, boo, no ghost, an empty sheet falls to the ground, I've
accumulated so many sheets, I could open a store.

## The Nightingale

Living on the edge of disaster, at home and possibly homeless,
the unreality of reality, anything can happen, ice melts in my
glass, in the world, I drink whatever comes to my lips, where is
the island that will not sink me, not the one we've been flooding,
when I survive a minor crisis, I wonder about all crises, they fall
before the fact of fate, I too will fall into its arms, surrender is not
capitulation, love is not a sublime trap, the nightingale is a drab,
brownish bird with a gorgeous voice at night.


## The Voice of This Life

"Poetry is a way of saying what one has difficulty feeling," some balk
at the language of the inexpressible, "poetry speaks the same language
I speak, but I don't understand it," poetry speaks the same language
and the same inexpressible reality, the inexpressible fights us at
every turn, it won't be tamed, when it does emerge, it speaks
in a voice that sounds foreign, unclear, clarity comes to the
unclear when the unclear becomes clear, the magic of poetry's
clarity becomes speaking beyond language to the soul, I want
clarity to choose its own language, some day, without speech,
I may come to speak the still, silent voice of life itself.

## I Sing Their Names

Not smart, dumb as a clod, soaking in the rain, drying out
in the sun, a great night's sleep catches on, I go through
the day in a lovely dream, I don't recall my life as a child,
memory is always young, I used to do things I have never
done, another life, just begun, looking in pieces for the whole,
I tried to discover who I was, walking on this path, others
running behind the trees, I sing their names, as if all the
armies turned to daffodils, puzzled by their training.

## This Voice, Not my Own

This voice, not my own, is a visitor from the truth of who I am,
a man alone, on a walk in the woods,  a bird lands by his feet,
I walked out of the world, into this life, the same but calmer,
I'm in the river of the moment, broken into eddies of time.

**She Wants a Baby**

She wants a baby, he doesn't, she's young, he's quite a bit older,
otherwise they are twins of agreement, in DC, there's no lobby for
the one who lives alone, not rugged but true, if one is truest to the spirit,
one can't be less true to all others, the true individual is not a power
player, he makes a list of who he says he is and presents it to her
eyes, not demands, separate from the soul it tries to describe.

All literature attempts the same thing, to tell the show of the soul,
failure of the species, we are never poet enough to truly rhyme
our being alive, alike as we are, we rhyme our sense of the other
to sound the same, so alike we think we're uniquely two as one,
but even oneness is diverse, this part of eternity is set apart from
that part of the same, she sees her baby daddy, he sees nothing
of either, she sees love in her loving, he sees love in love itself,
his will is free, hers is tied to the crib, each is about being born.

**A Farmer Constructs a Shed for His Cows**

A farmer constructs a shed for his cows, forgets a hat for his head,
a woman walks among flowers, without greeting, they know her,
in a room of separation, our common soul thrives in its company,
even though I don't know you, we are together in being apart,
in this town the rain comes down like individuals, contentedly,
in the dead of silence, your smile is all I know of you, I'm content.

### The Everyday Life of the Animals

Words together, an unsolvable Rubik's cube of understanding,
the moon disappears, hidden by a diaphanous display of vapors,
the trees make faces at me, I see them in their moving leaves,
I look like somebody that nobody looks at, until they see me,
I love my family, friends, the world, in no particular order,
the mighty mountains come tumbling down, one tiny dust
mote at a time, I once lived in anticipation of the past returning
remade,worship becomes routine in the everyday life of the animals.


### Unthought Thoughts

Unthought thoughts appear as poetry, they leap into life
from life unborn, thoughts unfelt or felt in feeling, yesterday,
become today's poem, cats cry for other cats in the night,
the next day they cry for their food.

## I Wanted to be Famous

I wanted to be famous, so I am, everyone ignores me, I can
tell I'm famous by the indifference I'm shown everywhere I go,
people see me and go about their business as if I didn't exist,
who knows what they are thinking, "Look at that famous guy,
leave him alone," I'm like you, I don't care about being famous,
it's great how we can pass each other without any recognition,
let this smile take the place of an autograph, you will have a
story to tell your grandchildren, and I will have this moment
of satisfaction in my fame, we will have truly known each
other, the fortunate ones, passing this glorious moment
in the timelessness of our brief time together.


## I'm Afraid to Write this Poem

I'm afraid to write this poem, I'm concerned with what
it might say, my friend says that when he doesn't know
what to say, he writes a poem, the desire to speak
overrides the absence of what might be said.

Absence of what might be said leans toward what might
be said in its place, absence of speaking is full of speech,
poetry reveals it, fear of the unknown lies safely at rest
in the unspoken poem, fear wants to be broken into pieces
of the known, shown in the light, the light of a poem is the
future home of darkly held fears, here it comes, the saying
of the unsaid, first known in the heart, I love my daughter,
there, it's been said, no more fear need abide within it.

## Denver Airport

Denver airport, thousands of fellow travelers, waiting, between,
then, roaring across the sky, the landscape below seems to drift
gently by, shaken and pelted with cold air, walking across the
sky, headed down, earth below lies solid as a rock, covered
with creatures in their lives, suspended animation, headed
home, rumble and roar, whine and sigh, screech and cry,
no silence at this speed.

Wide awake in the night, still in flight, silent wings at rest
by my side, ambitioned to be an angel, carried aloft by nothing
angelic, I love flying in metal and plastic, daily magic miracle,
take me home, airplane, I will no more disparage your obscene
glory, alighting on earth, the wheels down, scorching the tarmac,
still alive in the monster I love, home at last.

## Pawleys Island

I'm happy at the beach in the quiet roar, soft wind, still mind,
these old legs slow me down, until I find my place in motion,
the ocean is the horizon, edge of the world in my wide eyes,
I walk into the wind, a small hand outside a speeding car's
window, a small boat offshore, circled by a bevy of birds.

Sun has backlit the lowhanging clouds, a seagull walks brisky away,
the birds direct my steps, I trail their instincts to the water's edge,
a seagull stands on one leg, walks on two, stands on one, shakes
the other, I take steps on the sand, each step leaving its mark
ahead of the past, when these legs waver, they invent a dance,
a sunny jitterbug, a boy, in the surf in India, reappears in Carolina.

Poetry takes me out of myself, I am dog-eared familiar prose,
I think in history, walk in history, speak unhistoric time,
I record the life of timelessness inside the outside of my life,
yellow steps guide my way off the beach, toward this, these words.


## Walking on the Earth

Walking on the earth, going here to there, the sun warms the path
ahead, wooden palaces line the shore, empty lots between them
beg for more, waves crash into their mother, loving ocean of depth
and acceptance, these moments occur, ignorant of the clock in my
timeless seaside walk, I thought my attraction to all living things
had to do with love, one sandpiper picks, picks and picks, others
follow its earnest path.

## The Sun Soaks Each Human Document

The sun soaks each human document, turning its pages
to parchment, earth asks nothing of my feet, doesn't say stop,
move faster, run away, the dunes have grown grassy, a sparse
hairline on the ever-balding beach, steps to the beach stop at
the beach, lead back from the beach, life on the edge, Keats
at the Atlantic imagined stout Cortez at the Pacific, a man carries
his chair down to the shore in dreams of discovery, yesterday, I
crashed my bike, last night I bled on the sheets in my sleep, today,
I sit and stare, gazing at eternity, seashell in waves, I am tossed
and turned by nothing, endless blue, from which I, endless, grew.

## Awe Cares for the Awesome

A man stands waist deep in an ocean a million times greater
than he, I stand mere feet away from his audacious effrontery,
we fools, birds fly from sea to shore, from shore to sea, this is
their territory, they say, never turn your back on the ocean, so
I face its majesty, one cough in the throat of the ocean, and we
become our history, easy speculation plays in place of the fear of
the god called nature, the ocean does not care for me, I care for it.

Awe cares for the awesome, fear for the fearsome, love for
the eternal, the awesome, the fearsome, the eternal are my legacy,
I am water, I am air, I am earth, I am light, I am the dark, on the
edge of the ocean of my vanity and its simple truth, waves will
crash on my birthday, ten thousand years from now, without
a thought, I love the ocean, without a thought, we are the same,
I see my life without history, in awe and fear and love.

## This Last Morning at the Beach

This last morning at the beach, overcast, I walk on sand, toward
the sand, good morning, good morning, how are you, I'm good,
and you, I'm good, thank you, high tide has made the beach narrow,
few birds, few people, gray sky, gray beach, one seagull, then another,
standing watch, two sandpipers scout the surf, bare footprints, leaning
forward, large big toes dug in, as if in running, a man with a bag picks up
seashells, beachfront condos face the dawn, I turn, the wind resists my
leaving, I slowly make my way, I go, an old man, I'm older than I
pretend, not as old as I pretend.

## Lois McConnell

Lois McConnell never came fully into this life, her daughter said,
I recognized her, regardless, as we do, her daughter became a psychic
I fell in love with, as we all did, I attended the funerals of both women
where I sang their praises, in these recent years, I have loved peace
above all, mind free of passing affairs, the gentle rocking motion
of the earth, babies laughing in their cradles, to come fully into
this life is to awaken and laugh at its folly.

I have lost patience with patience, it seems to be waiting for something,
patience seems to care for arrival, it will wait for the cows, absence is
companion to patience, "Absence, I love you, please don't leave me,"
patience is never alone, what's missing fills its heart with painful joy,
patience knits pleasure from skeins of the absent fabric of the awaited,
patience competes with anxiety for the space of simple being, I have
no more time for patience or its crazy brother, impatience.

In ancient times, they wondered about the ones who came before,
I think of my youth when I thought of the nothingness from which
I came, when nothing thinks of nothing, it brings one back to the
moment of life, all history is bundled in thoughts of history but
lives in the moment, grandma loves her grandchildren, when they
come together as one love, I never miss anyone until I am with them,
then my heart aches, as if the moment of love, filled to bursting, bursts
into too much love, love is too much love, the heart is too much heart,
life is too much life, love pours into my heart, my heart breaks open
with life, I am alive.

To live with those I love, I sidestep the onslaught, easily done,
I hold my life at a distance and begin to miss my destruction,
I can't tell you how much I love you, it would tempt my ruination,
there is a name for the way I am, my act is a charade, I'm as erudite
as a scholar who forgets how to write his name, of course I remember
these tools when they come into play.

Creeley, my teacher, was brilliant, sometimes a drunk and sometimes an
asshole to his wife, he called her his muse, she rejected the job and took
up the calling, Bobbie Louise wrote the best tale of fried liver and onions
ever told, stillness is my master, as soon as I forget its brilliant dictates.

I'm sad when my young friend departs, I look out the window
as he leaves, a realtor, he makes good money doing it, he went to
medical school, left because of the human damage, sold insurance,
left because he could not help those who could not afford it, has a
small, beautiful daughter, he told her we have the same last name.

I observe my fellow humans like creatures at the watering hole,
how can I not love every one, moving through their remarkable lives,
Gary's on his way to teach at a Black Mountain music store, half the
nation wants its leader indicted for his criminal ways, an old man with
a breathing machine asks if he can share the table, and this morning,
Lucie read from the book, "Haikus for Jews," what's not to like?

As one center of the universe, I see all the other centers, if you feel
self-important, others will become less important, centers of life are
everywhere, the center of life is life itself, "I step into the ocean, and
the ocean is mine," says everyone who ever got wet, we drown in
ourselves when we forget to enjoy the communal swim.

I walk these woodland paths in my car on the streets between home
and here, the clouded sky seems like one cloud spread thin to block
the sun's advantage, everything is not one thing but parts of everything
else, aging has me humble, nothing else got me here as successfully,
to become humble is the secret to conquering the wiser world,
wisdom is the gentle outpouring of the spring of human kindness.

I walk my way through the dense woods of this concrete wilderness,
the full moon blackbird sings the light, here I am again, still in love
with life, all the ingredients of love are meted out before and after love
occurs, Marigold, Chrysanthemum, and Begonia can't recall their names.

I avoid the signs next to the paintings, I turn away from what I might
think, I have been in this cafe for ten years, it's become prosaic,
seventy-plus years in this body, its concomitant life of thought,
the faces are familiar, even those I've never seen before, always
changing, now mundane, I have seen the face in the mirror, but
when I love life itself, it blossoms, all is new, a river runs through
terror and boredom, taking itself to the sea, this great force of
renewal, from a trickle to its disappearance.

An accumulation of rain, floods, then destroys the homes of those ashore,
born on the Mississippi, I can't return to the same river, Huck Finn knew
the same story, he was imaginary, and so am I, the imagination of energy,
the power of the river, stirring, stirring, moving, moving, caressing the
banks of the body.

The bear scat found in the garden turns out to be buried black plastic,
the bear is real, invading the sanctuary of the backyard, the bear sees
no sanctuary but his own, from here to Tennessee, the black plastic
seems as aggressive, as sacrosanct, we honor the bear with our fear,
plastic is widespread, our fear subdued, the immediate rare, fearsome.

The ubiquitous is seldom seen, it's peaceful in the arboretum, away from
the no peace of these days, peace dogged my steps through the no peace
of a lifetime, so I wore its mask, the dog of peace followed me, constant,
faithful, loyal, asking nothing, occasionally, I would turn and look to see
its loving face raised, its face looked like my face, my face looked like
the face of a peaceful dog, I came to to recognize its face, my mask
slipped into acceptance, until one day, there was no mask, no dog,
no face but peace itself in my place.

Among the trees, alive in the peace of no peace, humility opens
recognition of the truth of everything, humility opens time to the
space for the fullness of being, I left my friends, my children, my
family, beliefs and ideas, I left them as my father left me, alone,
to find myself, I found no freedom, but a reasonable facsimile.

I abandoned myself to the vast empty universe, without hope, I let go
the parents of mind, the friends of heart, the self's family, and who I was,
before I was, plotted this course, I plotted its copy, the copy gave me no
release except a sort of ersatz freedom, I abandoned my abandonment.

A bird flies above the treeline, a fishermen hauls his long day's catch
home in a white plastic bucket, why does the world jump and crash,
why do birds not stop their flight in mid-air, there is something
normal here, something seen and told, reassurance of the rest.

A small dog held tight in the arms of its owner, precious prisoner,
this government, I'm at its mercy, not quite free enough to bow out,
things of the world dying, a leaf floods my eyes with green brilliance,
bamboo outgrows me in a day and a half, I'm like an ant in the grass,
I stay dry with my umbrella, but I miss the rain on my face.

This poem, so sweet and tart, I put it on the tongue of my heart,
the silent saint, in his meditation, strikes a blow for freedom's sake,
I write around, above, below and through this simple subject; stillness,
I wander into the garden, walk out of it and forget it's here, with all
these professional singers, I decide to sing my own song.

Searching for pearls, the pearl of wisdom reminds me to eat the
oyster, wise man in a hurry to make his life slow down, waits for the
lightning, Carolina wren crosses the road like a sacred cow among birds,
the emperor wears his clothes, hopelessly out of fashion and threadbare,
Mia, the old cat, lies in the street, patiently awaiting her massage, from
time to time, place to place, I wish Buddha were here, and then, he were.

I write these words for a certain reader who has yet to be named, I see,
between poems, an ad for furnishing one's apartment, an axe splits a tree's
trunk open, the aroma fills the snowy air, a shaggy dog twists its body in
a wild swirl on the couch, yesterday and tomorrow are easier to hold, yet
this moment lives, Shakespeare spoke of everything, making eloquence
of higher import, the air comes crowding in, until my breath is left
empty of all else.

"You go one way and then the other way," she said, standing where she stood, despair, that sharp spear, fades in the encounter with the air it cuts through, I hoped to take everything she said and make it mine for a year, I squeeze my life for a taste of its joy, I discover I am drowned, I exchange thoughts of death for a sigh, fair trade, neither losing its worth, long after the old sun has died, who will remember its brilliant light, Jesus embraced eternity, watching others invent its illusion, love is the imagined word for that which has no name to begin with, I stay in peace that breathes a life, earth addresses me with eyes of daffodils and rabbits leaping, my body a castle, a fortress, a mansion, I still want it all.

I fall in love, fall back in love, back into that from which I arise, I blow up life to giant, to legend, almost to the way it is, a bank of bushes by the road, a forest by the sea, flowers by a wall, an eagle soars in its sky, its eye not bravely spying, thinking of dining on a mouse, my brother died once, and then again, until his death became routine, my history is that of a dead man, my life's alive to the end of time, I stand beside myself, a king the royal soul, its low serf the mind, a volcano kills where once I stayed, this fragile life, a few miles, our teacher, gentle heart, stood before us young louts, reading "Richard Corey," in tears.

I'm told the heart is faint, its muscles strong, I long for heart and build a wall, the small trick of an animal brain to think it god and entertain itself, death no elephant in the room but a continual appearance, this dialog is stopped by the coming near of a human being, God spoke to me, just now, with his usual silent wordless presence, insects are whispering in my ear, to them a shout, "His blood is near!" this honey stings, its maker decrees, these sweets are borne among the bees, searching for a new word that has not yet made its name, this is the mind, standing on its nose, so it might smell a thought that rises above where it grows.

She sits by the sidewalk, twirling her hair, solving problems with a pen,
the despot sits close by, "a man of god," no dispute, without refute, I have
no more time for patience, or its crazy brother, love is too much love, the
heart is too much heart, life is too much life, stillness is my master, I walk
these woodland paths between home and here, the bear sees no sanctuary
but his own, from here to Tennessee.

A bird flies above the treeline, there's something normal here,
something seen and told, a sort of reassurance of the rest, pavillions
of thought, great circuses of available images, the state of the world,
the sun shining, somewhere it is raining hard, neither this nor that
is my finest work, I am lost alive, memory fades, wings grow,
I become something of nothing from what I was before.

**She Saw Me and Said So**

Steve Abhaya Brooks

copyright 2020

**ISBN:** 9781708502850

Zenman Books

Abhaya Books & Art

130 Evelyn Place

Asheville, NC 28801

steve@steveabhaya.com

steveabhaya.com

Made in USA - Kendallville, IN
1053736_9781708502850
03 16 2020 1258